The Worth of a Woman, Do You Know Your Value?

Volume # 1

Dr. Anthony Walton

The Worth of a Woman,
Do You Know Your Value?

Copyright © 2023 by Walton Publishing

All rights reserved.
No part of this book may be reproduced or transmitted in any form or by any means without written permission from the author.

ISBN: 978-1-7367209-5-0

Walton Publishing
Indianapolis, Indiana

Printed in USA

Many women in the Bible made their mark in their families, communities, country, and humanity. They were all quite intelligent and knew what they were doing. Although in certain situations some of them were uncompromising to their detriment. They had exceptional strength of character and were dauntlessly ready to take risks.

Emmanuel Q. & Bruce-Adjei
(Famous and Infamous Women In The Bible)

Dedication

I dedicate this book to my deceased mother Ethel Walton Pullins, who always encouraged me to strive to do and be my best. Her prayers and support were a vital part of my upcoming. She was a woman who prayed for me when I did not see my future but knowing her value and worth recognized the importance of praying for, encouraging, and supporting others.

To my lovely wife who always supports and encourages me, and is an inspiration to me as I continue to focus on achieving God's purpose in my life.

To my 6th grade teacher Dr. Lora Vann, and DeAnna Letsinger who also supported me in writing this book.

Finally to all the Mothers in different churches whether biological or spiritual moms who have poured into my life constantly lending me support and encouragement throughout the years.

Table of Contents

Purpose vi

Understanding Your Value 1

Mother Eve 11

Abigail the Intercessor 19

Tamar The Forgotten Widow 42

Tamar Plays the Harlot 47

Judah Acknowledges and Honors Tamar 50

Woman Caught in Act of Adultery 54

The Woman at the Well 61

The Widow's Mite 70

References 99

Purpose

This book is written as a tool to help to empower women to become the best they can be by recognizing their true self-worth and value.

I desire that after reading this book and seeing how many women have overcome similar obstacles in their lives it will inspire you to strive also.

As you read through this first volume of *The Worth Of A Woman, Do You Know Your Value?* my prayer is that it will strengthen your resolve to walk in your destiny and fulfill you.

I pray that it will strengthen your resolve to walk in your destiny allowing you to fulfill your God-given purpose.

THE WORTH OF A WOMAN, DO YOU KNOW YOUR VALUE?

Understanding Your Value

As a therapist, I have been fortunate enough to counsel many women, helping them to overcome grief, loss, abuse, heartbreak, and many of life's challenges they have had to face throughout their life.

Many of these women are bright, intelligent, beautiful, phenomenal, and gifted. Many have taken the time to invest in themselves, professionally as well as spiritually, but often I see a negative theme that repeatedly runs through these women's lives being insecure and for some having a negative sense of their worth. In part due to not having received the proper encouragement and support needed to develop a strong positive self-image. Because of this, they have come to not understand the importance they hold in life, and not knowing just how great value they possess, which will ultimately allow them to be able to build up themselves as well as others.

I am always moved with compassion as I hear story after story of gifted women who often settled for less than what they are worth and deserve because of them feeling uncomfortable in their skin. Often these women have negative self-images or are experiencing feelings of inadequacy due to trying to fulfill what is an unrealistic image of what they perceive as being their view of what a man expects how a woman should be.

As I talk with these clients encouraging and helping them to realize their true value and self-worth, I am amazed at how their view of themselves changes over time as they are encouraged to realize their true potential and begin to walk into their true purpose. For a woman to walk into her purpose she must first understand what her true purpose is. She must not look at herself in a critical or negative point of view focusing on all the flaws that she perceives she has.

Often both men and women, value themselves in relationships as to how they see themselves being viewed by others. They also focus on what they see as the perceptions of what other women and men may have of them.

A woman will look at what she sees as an amazing trait in another woman and will begin comparing herself to that woman. She may be admiring the beauty that she sees in the other woman, however, while she is admiring the outstanding traits she sees in the other woman that she would like to possess, at the same time the same woman she is admiring may also be admiring many traits she sees the woman that she is being admired by. The other woman may be wishing she had many of her traits. An example is a young petite average size young lady who shared with me how she admired a young lady who was tall about five feet and eleven inches, at the same time the taller woman shared with me how she often wished she was not as tall and more petite. She told me how she often felt so awkward and uncomfortable at times being the tallest woman in the room. So, as you can see, we often focus more on what we perceive as our flaws rather than having the ability to appreciate and celebrate our natural abilities, beauty, and gifts that are unique to us, and that others see in us.

Throughout history, we can find many situations, where women have made a tremendous impact on the lives of others, yet while doing this were not aware of their true value and wealth.

As you read this book, I would like to ask you the question "Do you know your self-worth?" I would like to encourage you to take an honest long and hard look at yourself as you answer this question. you are willing to look at yourself through the eyes of God, you will realize even with your imperfections you are a creature of beauty, a dear child of God made in His image, and have great value. You are a precious jewel.

Since the beginning of time, there are examples of women who have been reported to make wise decisions impacting many people, while some have made not-so-wise decisions simply because they were not able to identify their true worth. In many of these cases, they have had an influence on those around them for the good. However, unfortunately in some cases, some allowed their gifts to become a tool harming those around them simply because they either did not know their value or allowed themselves to manipulate the value they had for negative purposes.

Women are tremendous influencers that can build a community or tear it down. Anytime a woman is involved in anything, her participation in that activity can become a game changer. When that woman is a strong positive woman that is secure in herself and uses her natural God-given talent she can make a tremendous difference. On the other hand, a woman who loses focus of her true value and worth can create a negative atmosphere for herself as well as for those around her. Her actions can affect many generations to come.

I will address the question of "Do you know a Woman's Worth" throughout this book to allow the reader to assess themselves and answer the question as it relates to how they feel about themselves. My desire for those reading this book is that they will come to recognize and value all women.

From the beginning of time, as we know it, we will begin with Mother Eve. I will share how knowing or not knowing her worth made a tremendous impact on the world that you and I are still experiencing, the impact of it during our current time.

Many women have made a difference and they were not all women of renown. Some were just simple ordinary women who stepped up at the right time when they saw what needed to be done. The Bible talks about the children of Issachar:

> *"And of the children of Issachar, which were men that had an understanding of the times, to know what Israel ought to do; the heads of them were two hundred, and all their brethren were at their commandment."*
>
> ~ *I Chronicle 12:32 KJV*

This could also apply to many women who when called upon to make life-changing decisions are willing to respond appropriately, without hesitation.

Positive Affirmations

- I will use my God-given gifts to be a blessing to others
- I will always recognize my value in any situation
- I will not allow what others think of me to discourage me
- I will not allow anyone to make me feel less than who I am
- I will not speak negatively about myself
- I will not speak negatively to myself
- I will not depend on others to build me up
- I will not settle for less than what I feel I deserve

My Personal Affirmations

NOTES:

THE WORTH OF A WOMAN, DO YOU KNOW YOUR VALUE?

Mother Eve

After God created man, He looked at His creation and realized that man needed companionship, support, and help mate. So God took Eve from the man's rib and made a woman. Eve played a very essential role in the garden as she was to assist and aide Adam. Eve was so much needed that in her absence God declared that it was not good for man to be alone. Many men who are blessed to have a good woman working with and beside them will automatically become more successful with her than without her.

> *"And Adam called his wife Eve; because she was the mother of all living."*
>
> ~ Genesis 3:20 KJV

Eve had a special place as Adam recognized her as being the mother of all living. I believe Eve was beautiful inside and out, but not knowing her value found herself opening up to and allowing herself to be entertained by communicating with, and listening to the serpent. She lost focus on what had been shared with her by Adam regarding the freedom to eat any of the trees in the garden except for the tree of the knowledge of good and evil through listening to the cunningness of the serpent. She became enchanted with the subtle words of the serpent and began to lose consciousness of whom she was. Not knowing the gravity of her decision to eat the fruit and also encouraging Adam to eat the fruit as well. She was not aware of just how devastating it would be, and how her actions would come to change the course of history.

Whenever a person is not aware of the power they have they can be easily persuaded to relinquish that power to someone else.

Often men will take the women in their lives for granted and not realize their true value. Men must know the importance of both realizing and letting the women in their lives whether it be their wives, sisters, daughters, teachers, or even friends know just how valuable they are. He must first truly understand for himself the importance of their value. This can also apply to women. Too many women are unwilling or unaware of the importance of letting the men in their lives, as well as others, know their relationship has value.

There could be several reasons why Eve allowed herself to be seduced by satan. Many women desire to have a listening ear to share their thoughts and emotions with. It could be possible that Father Adam, like many men of today, became so involved in what he was doing that he failed to have an emotional conversation or connection with Eve over time. "Women wish men knew the importance of just listening. They do not have to try to solve all their problems, but be there with a supportive listening ear". *"The Window to Understanding and Building Healthy Relationships"(Walton p.25).*

For a woman to be heard and understood is one of the most important things she can experience in any relationship. Women are very complex individuals and will normally allow you to know a portion of what she is thinking and feeling in any relationship. Only when they feel you are truly concerned enough about them to listen and hear what is truly on their heart as you allow them to freely express themselves that they will fully open up and completely and uninhibitedly share their heart with you. Men must realize just how important it is for a woman to be heard. If you really want a powerful connection with a woman, be willing to be sensitive enough to hear her inner thoughts, desires, hopes, and dreams and allow her to express them without being judged, but rather by you having an attitude of acceptance.

Positive Affirmations

- I will be careful who I lend my ear to
- Before acting I will consider the consequences of my actions
- I will value all the relationships I have
- I will strive to improve my relationships with others

My Personal Affirmations

_____

_____

_____

_____

_____

_____

_____

_____

_____

_____

_____

_____

_____

_____

_____

_____

NOTES:

Abigail the Intercessor

"And when Abigail saw David, she hasted, and lighted off the ass, and fell before David on her face, and bowed herself to the ground,
And fell at his feet, and said, Upon me, my lord, upon me let this iniquity be: and let thine handmaid, I pray thee, speak in thine audience, and hear the words of thine handmaid.
Let not my lord, I pray thee, regard this man of Belial, even Nabal: for as his name is, so is he; Nabal is his name, and folly is with him: but I thine handmaid saw not the young men of my lord, whom thou didst send.
*Now therefore, my lord, as the L*ORD *liveth, and as thy soul liveth, seeing the L*ORD *hath withholden thee from coming to shed blood, and from avenging thyself with thine own hand, now let thine enemies, and they that seek evil to my lord, be as Nabal.*
And now this blessing which thine handmaid hath brought unto my lord, let it even be given unto the young men that follow my lord.
*I pray thee, forgive the trespass of thine handmaid: for the L*ORD *will certainly make my lord a sure house; because my lord fighteth the battles of the L*ORD, *and evil hath not been found in thee all thy days.*
*Yet a man is risen to pursue thee, and to seek thy soul: but the soul of my lord shall be bound in the bundle of life with the L*ORD *thy God; and the souls of thine enemies, them shall he sling out, as out of the middle of a sling.*
*And it shall come to pass when the L*ORD *shall have done to my lord according to all the good that he hath spoken concerning thee, and shall have appointed thee ruler over Israel;*
That this shall be no grief unto thee, nor offense of heart unto my lord, either that thou hast shed blood causeless, or

that my lord hath avenged himself: but when the LORD shall have dealt well with my lord, then remember thine handmaid.
And David said to Abigail, Blessed be the LORD God of Israel, which sent thee this day to meet me:
And blessed be thy advice, and blessed be thou, which hast kept me this day from coming to shed blood, and from avenging myself with mine own hand.
For in very deed, as the LORD God of Israel liveth, which hath kept me back from hurting thee, except thou hadst hasted and come to meet me, surely there had not been left unto Nabal by the morning light any that pisseth against the wall.
So David received of her hand that which she had brought him, and said unto her, Go up in peace to thine house; see, I have hearkened to thy voice, and have accepted thy person."
~ *1 Samuel 25:23-35 KJV*

The old saying used to be behind every good man is a good woman. But I believe a good woman is a lady that exhibits the wisdom to position herself in the right place at the right time for the right reason. This woman will have the confidence to support others without having to feel she must take the lead. Many women have been in marriages, relationships, jobs, and even in the church, where their true value may not have ever been recognized or appreciated. A good woman will add value to her husband or to whatever she has been tasked to do.

Abigail

Abigail stands out for several reasons. As a woman of beauty, brains, wisdom, and discernment, she counsels David and prophesies regarding his kingship. Because of the wisdom and humility, she showed toward David, it was the major factor leading to causing David to spare her husband's life. I believe this was instrumental in David, after the death of her husband, choosing her to be his wife. He could see the love and support she showed toward her husband even though she realized his lack of wisdom. Her character shows us an example that women of God can be humble, wise, and diplomatic.

Abigail represents the kind of woman who seeks to cover and protect her man even in the worst of situations.

Many men would love to have a wife like Abigail, but it takes a unique woman who has the love of God to be able to cover her husband in the worst of situations. Abigail was an asset to her husband recognizing his weakness but having the love and character to cover him and support him even as she was able to recognize the weaknesses he possessed.

A powerful woman will complement the man or people in her life making them stronger and more successful by simply using her God-given strength to build him and others around her.

Many men desire the kind of woman Abigail was, but like Nabal, too often, many men who are looking for this kind of woman will have her in their life, but sadly, will take her for granted. They may not know just how valuable she is and just how much she adds to his life, until often, it is too late. Men must learn to recognize the value of the women in their lives and learn to not only say they appreciate them but, also go above and beyond to show them just how much they are appreciated!

Positive Affirmations

- When you do the right thing you will be noticed

- As I cover the ones I love, God will cover me

- As you bless the stranger, God will give you a great blessing in return

- God is not unrighteous to forget your labor of love

- I will do the right thing for the right reason

My Personal Affirmations

_____
_____
_____
_____
_____
_____
_____
_____
_____
_____
_____
_____
_____
_____
_____
_____

NOTES:

"And Judah took a wife for Er his firstborn, whose name was *Tamar.*
And Er, Judah's firstborn, was wicked in the sight of the LORD; and the LORD slew him.
And Judah said unto Onan, Go in unto thy brother's wife, and marry her, and raise up seed to thy brother.
And Onan knew that the seed should not be his; and it came to pass, when he went in unto his brother's wife, that he spilled it *on the ground, lest that he should give seed to his brother.*
And the thing which he did displeased the LORD: wherefore he slew him also."
~ Genesis 37:6-10 KJV

An Unidentified Women

"And a certain woman, which had an issue of blood twelve years,

And had suffered many things of many physicians, and had spent all that she had, and was nothing bettered, but rather grew worse,

When she had heard of Jesus, came in the press behind, and touched his garment.

For she said, If I may touch but his clothes, I shall be whole.

And straightway the fountain of her blood was dried up, and she felt in her body that she was healed of that plague."

~ Mark 5:25-29 KJV

This story references this woman as being a certain woman. This does not diminish her importance but rather is indicative of a woman who may not be recognized personally by others but has been able to receive the favor of God. Her name, ethnicity, financial or social status is not mentioned and is not what is most important. This certain woman can be indicative of any number of women who find themselves being challenged by problems in life that appear to be insurmountable. The woman's name is omitted because she symbolizes any number of women finding themselves being in need and struggling to find the help needed to overcome their affliction.

Many women find themselves questioning their identity due to feeling as though they are unimportant because of their circumstances. You may be struggling financially, emotionally, socially, or even physically as this woman was. What is important to realize is, to do as this woman did, and that is to keep moving forward in life not giving up until you can overcome whatever challenges you are facing.

It is important to realize that in the end it was not her name, social or economic status that Jesus recognized but the faith she had that making a connection with Jesus would change her life forever.

Some women, unfortunately, allow their present circumstances and their view of themselves to become an obstacle to growing and establishing long-lasting healthy relationships. Your present circumstance does not ultimately determine your future. You must be willing to see past whatever you are faced with and see yourself growing and developing into the woman you desire to become.

I see this story as a powerful revelation of a woman of faith. The Bible describes her simply as a certain woman. It does not go into much detail regarding her. I believe the woman was unspecified because she could have been a mother, a widow, or several different titles. However, it does state:

- She had a Blood Condition
- She had been seen and suffered by many physicians
- She had spent all her Money
- She was not getting any better
- She heard of Jesus
- She had Faith that if she could connect with Jesus she would be Healed
- She was Healed of Her Plague

This woman was hemorrhaging which meant that she was most likely in a weakened state. Where many would have given up, this certain woman tried everything she knew to find healing for her body.

Many women are resilient and fighters refusing to give up regardless of the odds against them. I remember watching my mother as she was often sick and rather than give up would focus her energy on the welfare of her children and then on herself.

Many women go day in and day out suffering from one issue or another but refuse to give up.

I find it interesting that this woman did not have a name but the emphasis was on her struggle and her desire to find relief. Her faith caused her to continue to pursue forward in search of a solution to her problem.

Even though this woman was not recognized by name her story was a powerful one in that she received what she needed because she placed her faith in Jesus.

This certain woman could be any woman with any of the many issues as well as challenges affecting their physical as well as mental state.

Many women are sensitive individuals, and I don't mean that to imply weakness but to say they have a keen awareness of themselves as well as others around them in most situations.

Because a woman may have an issue in one area of her life does not mean she does not have value in other areas of her life. Many women go through an array of emotions that constantly causes them to second-guess themselves.

I remember a client who was highly educated and had a wealth of resources. However, due to the demands of her personal and work life, often found herself constantly being stressed out. Even though she was highly successful in her business life she saw herself as a failure in her personal life.

This woman's issue was that of low self-esteem. She could not appreciate the success in her business life, due to feeling there was something wrong with her because her personal life appeared to be a failure.

After many sessions, we were able to realize that a big part of her problem was an inability to be connected to the right person. She, like many women, and men as well, was uncomfortable with not having someone in her life. We must learn to be comfortable with ourselves whether we are with someone or alone.

This woman in the Bible went from physician to physician, but as with a number of my clients, found herself going from one man to another in search of acceptance and healing. Many men I have counseled have spent a great deal of money trying to find the person who will give them a sense of fulfillment. We must come to realize that personal fulfillment must come from within. It involves the ability to accept ourselves even with our many flaws. We must be able to recognize our flaws and take steps to correct them.

With women, as well as with men, the true satisfaction they have is when they are willing to seek after and pursue Jesus just as the woman in the story.

Many women are suffering in silence not being understood because of their complex nature. This bible does not state whether or not this woman was aware of the cause of her problem, but merely talks about the symptoms of her problem. There are times when the solution to your problem may be a simple fix and on the other hand, it may require more than just a simple fix. Whatever problems you may find yourself facing, do not be afraid to get the help that you need.

I had a client who had several issues, and because she had so many issues she found herself being overwhelmed by them all. I advised her that we would have to address her issues one step at a time. Often we can not see the trees due to the vastness of the forest. If you are having feelings of being overwhelmed by life, I would encourage you to take a step back and address one issue at a time.

When you step back and look at some of your issues, you may not be the problem, but it is how the circumstances have happened in your life. I encourage you to take a long hard honest look at yourself and be willing to address the issues you have in your life. Doing this will help you in overcoming your challenges so that you can be the best version of yourself that you can be.

As my client was able to address her issues one step at a time, we were able to reduce her stress and anxiety allowing her to look at herself from a more positive perspective. Once she was able to see herself from a positive perspective it allowed her to not only grow but to flourish in her personal as well as her professional life.

It is important to not give up on yourself or your condition, but as the woman with the issue of blood, after she had tried many other options to find relief for her issues, but her faith in Jesus. For many men and women, the key to their deliverance is by making the right choice to put their faith in God, and to make this a priority in their life.

"But seek ye first the kingdom of God, and his righteousness; and all these things shall be added unto you."

~ Matthew 6:33 KJV

THE WORTH OF A WOMAN, DO YOU KNOW YOUR VALUE?

Positive Affirmations

- I will carry all my issues to God
- I will not give up on myself no matter what issues I have
- No matter how difficult life gets I will press forward
- I will be honest about myself regarding my issues
- I will never abandon my faith in God
- I will make myself a priority

My Personal Affirmations

NOTES:

Tamar The Forgotten Widow

The story of Tamar is an interesting story of a woman who was made a promise but later forgotten about or just neglected in general. Tamar the daughter-in-law of Judah is an example of just how many men of that time viewed women as it also demonstrates how little of a value the men placed on women at that time.

Tamar the wife of Judah's son Er, who had died. The Bible states that:

Er was wicked in the sight of the Lord"; the Lord slew him.

Levirate marriage:

Levirate marriage (from the Latin word *levir*, meaning "husband's brother") – this institution safeguards the childless widow within the tribal framework. According to Deuteronomy 25:5-10, this duty falls on the surviving brother-in-law (Deut 25:5-10). In the story of Judah, however, the responsibility falls not only on the brother of the deceased but on other males in the family, in this case, the father. This likely reflects the old tribal institution of the *go'el*, as seen in the Book of Ruth.

It was the custom at that time that the responsibility of the next of kin was to care for the widow. This would have made Judah's son Onan the next in line to become her husband, which is what would have happened, but unfortunately, he died also.

And Judah said unto Onan, Go in unto thy brother's wife, and marry her, and raise up seed to thy brother. 9 And Onan knew that the seed should not be his; and it came to pass, when he went in unto his brother's wife, that he spilled it on the ground, lest that he should give seed to his brother.

~ *Genesis 38:8-10 KJV*

Judah's son Onan also displeased the Lord when he was to continue the lineage by giving Tamar his seed. However, he chose rather instead to spill his seed onto the ground.

*And Onan knew that the seed should not be his; and it came to pass, when he went in
unto his brother's wife, that he spilled it on the ground, lest that he should give seed to his brother. And the thing which he did displeased the LORD: wherefore he slew him also.*

~ Genesis 38:11 KJV

> *Then said Judah to Tamar his daughter in law, Remain a widow at thy father's house, till Shelah my son be grown: for he said, Lest peradventure he die also, as his brethren* did. *And Tamar went and dwelt in her father's house.*
> *~ Genesis 38:11 KJV*

After the death of Onan Judah's next son Shelah was promised to Tamar. Shelah was not of age to marry Tamar so she was requested to remain with her family until Shelah was of age and then she would be given to him to become her next husband.

Tamar stayed true to her commitment to maintaining herself as a widow waiting on Shelah to become of age to marry her. It appears that she had been forgotten about because the Bible does not mention anything regarding a marriage between Tamar and Shelah.

Tamar Plays the Harlot

> *"And it came to pass about three months after, that it was told Judah, saying, Tamar, thy daughter in law hath played the harlot; and also, behold, she is with child by whoredom. And Judah said, Bring her forth, and let her be burnt.*
> *~ Genesis 38:24 KJV*

After some time had passed, Tamar was informed that Judah did not keep his promise to her of having her to becoming the wife of Shelah.

What is important to note is because of the culture of that time, many women did not have the resources to provide for themselves and needed the support of their husbands if they were married to provide for them as well as to be their cover and to continue the bloodline by having a child by the next of kin. However, after a period of time, it was as if she was just forgotten about.

Because Tamar was overlooked she devised a method of having Judah fulfill the responsibility of allowing her to have a child by the male blood relative to her deceased husband.

Men must recognize the value of a woman and not see her merely as a fleshly object but as a kind, loving, and intelligent person to be loved, appreciated, and respected. Judah was not true to his promise to Shelah and when he heard that she was pregnant did not take into consideration for one minute the series of events that had left her as a widow all this time.

Many men do not look at their actions and see them as being wrong but are quick to judge and condemn the actions of women even if they are guilty of the same thing. To say there is a double standard is a gross understatement.

Judah decides to go and have fun and sow his wild oats and encounters a beautiful woman who he thought was a harlot (Tamar) not knowing it was his daughter-in-law. She must have been a beautiful woman because he was willing to give her almost anything to get with her. She asked for his signet, his bracelets, and the staff in his hand that he leaned on. She then consented to let him connect with her sexually.

Three months after his encounter with Tamar he hears that she is pregnant and goes to confront her so that he could put her to death by setting her on fire. But Tamar shows her wisdom in that she exposes him for who he was as well as not being a man of his word.

Tamar here represents a woman who shows more wisdom than her father-in-law by securing the items she requested from him. This allowed her to confirm the relationship she had with her father-in-law and to also prove that he was the father of her child.

Although Tamar had been forgotten she found a way to accomplish what was promised to her.

Judah Acknowledges and Honors Tamar

"And Judah acknowledged them, and said, She hath been more righteous than I; because that I gave her not to Shelah my son. And he knew her again no more."
Genesis 38:26 KJV

Many women or wise and very strategic when it comes to getting what they want. In this case, Tamar was wise and strategic in getting what was promised to her.

Many women have been made promises by men that were broken but unlike what Tamar had to go through to receive what was promised to them if they will go to God and trust him he will give them the desires of their heart.

"Delight thyself also in the Lord*: and he shall give thee the desires of thine heart."*

~ Psalms 37:4 KJV

Judah eventually acknowledges his negligence in not keeping his word to Tamar and confirms that what she had done was a result of him not fulfilling his promise to her.

"And Judah acknowledged them, and said, She hath been more righteous than I; because that I gave her not to Shelah my son. And he knew her again no more."

~ Genesis 38:26 KJV

My Personal Affirmations

_____

_____

_____

_____

_____

_____

_____

_____

_____

_____

_____

_____

_____

_____

NOTES:

Woman Caught in Act of Adultery

Just as in Biblical times there still is a disparity between the way men and their actions are viewed in relationship to how the same actions of women are viewed. In the article "How Culture Impacts Our Value Of Women" written by Dr. Shawn Andrews, she writes:

"family culture, based on our race or ethnicity, is equally as powerful and starts just as early. In many cultures, women are expected to be responsible for things that men are not. And, there are more pressures put on girls and women to look and behave in certain ways."

It seems in some ways we are far removed from the biblical days but in many ways even though women have come a long way there is a disparity in the value that is placed on them. When we look at the corporate world and labor force in general we can see that the pay for women is much less than for men who are doing the same job even thou many women have been proven to have to work harder for a lesser amount of pay.

I believe Jesus recognized this disparity in his response toward the men who brought to Him the woman who was supposedly caught in the act of adultery.

> *And the scribes and Pharisees brought unto him a woman taken in adultery; and when they had set her in the midst,*
> *They say unto him, Master, this woman was taken in adultery, in the very act.*
> *Now Moses in the law commanded us, that such should be stoned: but what sayest thou?*
> *This they said, tempting him, that they might have to accuse him. But Jesus stooped down, and with his finger wrote on the ground, as though he heard them not.*
> *So when they continued asking him, he lifted up himself, and said unto them, He that is without sin among you, let him first cast a stone at her.*
>
> John 8:2-7 KJV

On the surface, these men appeared to be concerned about the woman not following the law. It appeared they were doing their civic duties of having this woman be held accountable for her sinful actions. As we dive a little bit further into their actions we can see several serious missing components.

- The man was nowhere to be found
- How were they made aware of the act of adultery being made
- Why did they not bring the man also
- How were they even able to verify what had happened
- What were their motives

This woman symbolizes many women who have been judged for their actions by those whose sins have been covered up but or so quick to uncover someone else's sins.

The Bible states that this woman was caught in the act of adultery but other than the testimony of a few self-righteous men who wanted to exact the death penalty on her without considering their ungodly deeds we can never know the true story.

I am not saying that this woman was not adulterous but am pointing out the fact that Jesus valued her life so much that he stood in the gap for her by asking the men:

But Jesus stooped down, and with his *finger wrote on the ground,* as though he heard them not.

So when they continued asking him, he lifted up himself, and said unto them, He that is without sin among you, let him first cast a stone at her.
John 8:7 KJV

This was so powerful in that it showed that Jesus recognized that her value was no less than that of the men who had brought her to Jesus expecting, for whatever reason, to have the pleasure of seeing her put to death.

Jesus did not dismiss her sin; He granted her a reprieve. He gave her the freedom to go, and He implicitly recognized that the choices she had yet to make would determine the shape of her future. (Sue and Larry Richards - 1999)

My Personal Affirmations

NOTES:

The Woman at the Well

"And he must need go through Samaria."

John 4:4 KJV

This scripture speaks of Jesus going to Samaria on what appears to be a mission. What could be so important that the scripture states "he must needs go through Samaria", could it be that he had to have an encounter with a woman who did not know her self-worth?

As he is on his journey, he encounters a woman alone by herself at the well. She is unaccompanied by anyone and as she is about to draw water for herself, he asks her to give him a drink. This woman may have just seen Jesus as another man wanting something from her. This woman had no doubt suffered many disappointments from the various men in her life.

She probably started the day off thinking it would just be another day of isolation and loneliness, unaware that an encounter with Jesus was about to change her life forever.

This Woman was different from the other women. Many ladies have insecurities and issues when they feel they are different from other women, while at the same time trying to blend in or act like other women. Attempting to blend in prevents them from being their unique self. When a woman attempts to blend in she prevents herself from exhibiting the true God-individual nature that she has and also deprives others of benefitting from this God-given uniqueness.

It could also be assumed that this woman may have been considered an outcast. No doubt others in the city knew of her past. Many of the women may have been afraid to associate with her. They may have even been fearful of her getting too close to them and she possibley stealing their husbands from them.

This woman may have suffered from low self-esteem questioning her self-worth due to the choices in life she had made.

For many women, the only form of validating themselves is by flaunting their beauty, and sexuality. When a man is drawn to their sexual appeal, it gives them a false sense of self-worth. Over time, these women come to realize a physical attraction is only temporary and can not create a long-lasting healthy relationship.

I have had clients ask me *"What is wrong with me? I find myself going from one relationship to another. Just when I think I'm in a good relationship something happens and he leaves me."* Many of these ladies have formed attachment issues that cause them to self-sabotage their relationships due to past experiences. Attachment issues are when a person has difficulty forming and maintaining close relationships. This can be due to a variety of factors, such as being raised in an environment where there was little love or stability, being abused or neglected as a child, or having parents who were distant or unavailable.

In many cases involving an unhealthy attachment style, I have been successful in helping both men and women in working through this once they are aware of the problem.

Like many women, the woman at the well may have been ashamed of her past and the poor choices in life she had made, as well as the many bad relationships of her past.

As Jesus spoke with her she began to have a theological discussion regarding the well and its history. I believe the more she communicated with him the more she realized there was something different about him. Previously she may have thought he could potentially be husband number six since she had been married five times before and was now living with a man. Many women feel that they can only have value as they attach themselves to another man. Many women will hold on to a man for fear of being alone even if they know this is not the right man for them.

As Jesus continues the conversation he seemingly sees right through her and can touch her in a way that no other man in her life had done. When a woman gets close to Jesus he will help her to understand who she really is and what her true purpose is. This woman was so touched that she proclaimed to the others:

"Come, see a man, which told me all things that ever I did: is not this the Christ?"
John 4:29 KJV

This woman left a changed woman, all because she talked to and connected with Jesus. If you are facing challenges in your life. I would encourage you to get connected with Jesus and ask him to give you the direction you need.

> *"Trust in the LORD with all your heart*
> *and lean not on your own understanding;*
> *in all your ways submit to him,*
> *and he will make your paths straight"*
> *Proverbs 3:5-6 NIV*

Positive Affirmations

- When and If I fall or fail God, I will acknowledge that I serve a loving and forgiving God
- Even when I am alone I will always trust that God is with me
- I will not look for a man to validate who I am
- I will not just settle for any man in my life
- I will not allow myself to view myself as being unworthy of love

My Personal Affirmations

_____

_____

_____

_____

_____

_____

_____

_____

_____

NOTES:

The Widow's Mite

And he looked up, and saw the rich men casting their gifts into the treasury.

And he saw also a certain poor widow casting in thither two mites.

And he said, Of a truth I say unto you, that this poor widow hath cast in more than they all:

For all these have of their abundance cast in unto the offerings of God: but she of her penury hath cast in all the living that she had.
                                                    Luke 21:1-4 KJV

Society places a lot of value on material things. We often judge people by what they wear, the car they drive, their banking account, their looks as well as many other materialistic values.

Many people are eager to entertain someone who they perceive as having it going on, someone we see as flossing. But in the eyes of God who looks at the heart, he does not judge us in any way by what we have. After all, we must realize that all we have accomplished is all by the grace and mercies of a loving God.

"But the LORD said unto Samuel, Look not on his countenance, or on the height of his stature; because I have refused him: for the LORD seeth not as man seeth; for man looketh on the outward appearance, but the LORD looketh on the heart."

1 Samuel 16:7 KJV

In the eyes of many, this woman who is one of many women in the Bible not mentioned by name, appears to be unimportant. To others, she may have been an insignificant widow seemingly of not much value to anyone. I'm sure as others looked at her as they went their way, they may have passed by without even noticing her, or if they did notice her, they may have just passed by without taking the time to speak.

We often judge people by their social class and in doing so I wonder how many good people we have passed by who could very well add value to our lives.

"Be not forgetful to entertain strangers: for thereby some have entertained angels unawares."

Hebrews 13:2 KJV

I have included this story because many women may feel like this unnamed widow who appeared to have very little to offer anyone.

Many women are so critical of themselves, their looks, their awkwardness, and their material limitations that they fail to realize that every man does not simply look at women for what they have to offer or what they have materialistically. Many women place a value on themselves according to vanity. This is why the cosmetic industry makes billions of dollars a year focusing on women who want to stand out in the crowd.

According to a report from retail analytics firm Edited, a retail intelligence company headquartered in London, England with offices worldwide including New York and Texas, the beauty industry is valued at 532 billion dollars. The industry, which is on a rapid upward trajectory, appears to want women to feel that they will not be noticed or accepted unless they somehow must enhance themselves.

The reason I find this story, which could easily have gone unnoticed, is because this woman who appeared not to have anything of great wealth was recognized by Jesus not because of the abundance of what she had materially, but because of the abundance of her heart.

Some superficial women are willing to give only for gain out of a portion of what they have, but a woman who has a loving, kind, and giving heart that will give you her all, is a woman of great value. This story reflects how Jesus placed a premium not on what she had but measured how she was willing to give *all* she had.

Many women have loving hearts and are willing to give all they have, the problem is she must not give all she has to just anyone, but must through prayer, seek God for whom she can give her all. Never give your all to someone who will not value you for who and what you are. When you give your all to the wrong man you will end up full of hurt and disappointment.

You may be like this widow who appeared to not have much to give anyone, but I encourage you to continue to put your trust and faith in God. When you do this, God will send the right man along who will recognize your worth and will be accepting of you just as you are.

Positive Affirmations

- I will always give God my best
- God does not judge me out of my abundance of resources but rather out of the abundance of my heart

- I will not compare myself to other women
- I will strive to be the best version of myself that I can be
- I will not allow others to make me feel that I am less than who I am

My Personal Affirmations

NOTES:

The Virtuous Woman

Who can find a virtuous woman? for her price is far above rubies.

The heart of her husband doth safely trust in her, so that he shall have no need of spoil.

She will do him good and not evil all the days of her life

She seeketh wool, and flax, and worketh willingly with her hands.

She is like the merchants' ships; she bringeth her food from afar.

She riseth also while it is yet night, and giveth meat to her household, and a portion to her maidens.

She considereth a field, and buyeth it: with the fruit of her hands she planteth a vineyard.

She girdeth her loins with strength, and strengtheneth her arms.

She perceiveth that her merchandise is good: her candle goeth not out by night.

She layeth her hands to the spindle, and her hands hold the distaff.

She stretcheth out her hand to the poor; yea, she reacheth forth her hands to the needy.

She is not afraid of the snow for her household: for all her household are clothed with scarlet.

She maketh herself coverings of tapestry; her clothing is silk and purple.

Her husband is known in the gates, when he sitteth among the elders of the land.

She maketh fine linen, and selleth it; and delivereth girdles unto the merchant.

Strength and honour are her clothing; and she shall rejoice in time to come.

She openeth her mouth with wisdom; and in her tongue is the law of kindness.

She looketh well to the ways of her household, and eateth not the bread of idleness.

Her children arise up, and call her blessed; her husband also, and he praiseth her.

Many daughters have done virtuously, but thou excellest them all.

Favour is deceitful, and beauty is vain: but a woman that feareth the LORD, she shall be praised.

Give her of the fruit of her hands; and let her own works praise her in the gates.

I cannot conclude this book without focusing on this passage in the Bible. It is normally quoted in many churches on Mother's Day. But as we take a closer look at these verses it demonstrates the qualities of a God-given woman. I could go verse by verse but in this book, I would like to share a few excerpts from this chapter as it discusses the virtues of a Godly woman.

This passage starts by asking the question of who can find a virtuous woman. This implies to me that a virtuous woman is like a rare diamond that is hard to find. This could be interpreted as who has the wisdom and desire to be able to find and recognize this type of woman.

Many men say they want this type of woman but are not willing and or not patient enough to take the time to patiently find this kind of woman. This is why far too many marriages end with divorce. Many men become impatient and are more concerned about the vanity of a woman rather than taking the time to find a God-kind of woman.

> *"He who finds a wife finds what is good and receives favor from the* L ORD*." Proverbs 18:22 NIV*

Let's look at this for a moment. It says he finds what is good.

There are some men and women who have no idea of the true worth of a good woman. The Bible speaks regarding a wife, a good wife will be making one of the greatest if not the greatest investments in the life of a man.

Because a Godly man will take the time to patiently search out and find the right wife that God has designed for him, the scriptures tell us that this man will obtain the favor of God.

Let's take a look at the word *favor:*

Truth #1: God's Favor *is* God's grace.

We have been saved by the Grace of God

Truth #2: God's favor affects every area of life.

God's favor has taken care of everything you will ever need—spirit, soul, and body. Every part of your life is impacted by the grace and favor of God.

Truth #3: God began showing you His favor even before you were born again.

"But God showed his great love for us by sending Christ to die for us while we were still sinners." – Romans 5:8

Truth #4: God's favor surrounds you continually.

"For You, O Lord will bless the righteous; with favor, You will surround him as with a shield."

–Psalm 5:12, *NKJV*

This favor from God that a man will receive when he finds a good wife can not be unestimated. When a man finds and marries a God-like woman these blessings will come along with her.

A godly woman is priceless. You can not put a price tag on this type of woman. Some men, unfortunately, will not recognize this until they meet a Godless woman, who does not add any value to his life. Next, the Bible states:

"She will do him good and not evil all the days of her life"

This type of woman will add significant value to her husband's life. She will not try to take away from him or distract him by competing with him but will focus on helping him to accomplish his desired goals. A woman who knows her value does not feel threatened by her husband's accomplishments but will celebrate all of his achievements. She desires to do him good as well as his desire should be the same for her. This kind of woman is a giving, caring, and sharing woman with a heart after God.

Women are God's greatest gift to man. When God created woman he recognized that man was incomplete without her. Whether as a mate, friend, co-worker, church member, or friend, a Godly woman always adds value to the relationship.

Positive Affirmations

- I will support my husband and those people that God has placed in my life

- I will focus on being the best I can be

- I will strive to help others

- I will make wise decisions

- I will never respond hastily without first thinking out my actions

My Personal Affirmations

NOTES:

NOTES:

Positive Attributes of A Woman

- Generosity and desire to be of help whenever she can
- Attentive listening before speaking her mind
- Attracting unconditional love by giving it freely
- Valuing people and relationships more than material things
- Confidence and lack of petty jealousy
- Dependability by being true to her word
- Honesty

12 Qualities of a Good Woman You Should Look For:

1. • She has Great Integrity
2. • She is nurturing
3. • She isn't the jealous type
4. • She is forgiving
5. • She is willing to show Compassion for others
6. • She is fun to be around
7. • She displays great kindness
8. • Encouraging you and others
9. • She displays loyalty
10. • She looks to better herself and others
11. • She is an appreciative woman
12. • She does not seek to change you

THE WORTH OF A WOMAN, DO YOU KNOW YOUR VALUE?

I Display the Following Qualities

_____

_____

_____

_____

_____

_____

_____

_____

_____

_____

_____

_____

_____

_____

_____

I Would Like to Display the Following Qualities

_____

_____

_____

_____

_____

_____

_____

_____

_____

_____

_____

_____

Qualities Than Men Find Unattractive in a Woman

- **Talking Without Listening**

- **Egocentric**

- **Pessimistic**

- **Always having to be right**

- **Dishonesty**

- **Judgmental**

- **Critical**

- **Selfish**

- **No Self-Control**

- **Unwilling to Compromise**

- **Possessive**

- **Jealous**

- **Argumentative**

7 MISCONCEPTIONS MEN HAVE ABOUT WOMEN

1. Women Don't Know What They Want

2. Women Are Hard To Understand

3. Women Are always Indecisive

4. All Women Are The Same

5. All Women Are Only Attracted To Money

6. Women Are Hard To Please

7. Most Women Can't Be Trusted

I include this section because men must learn to have a positive view of women for them to be able to establish healthy relationships.

Some of the topics to be discussed in Volume # 2

- **A woman and her emotional connections.**

- **The influence of a woman**

- **The vulnerability of a woman**

- **The Heart of a Woman**

- **The Sacrifice of a Woman**

- **God's Woman Chosen For This Season**

References

Andrews, S. (2020, April 6). *How Culture Impacts Our Value Of Women.* https://www.drshawnandrews.com/articles/how-culture-impacts-our-value-of-women

Biron, B. (2019, July 9). *Beauty Becomes a $532 Billion Dollar Industry.* https://www.businessinsider.com/beauty-multibillion-industry-trends-future-2019-7

Emmanuel, Q., & Bruce-Adjei, M. (2020). *Famous And Infamous Women In The Bible.*

MacArthur, J. (2005). *Twelve extraordinary women: How God shaped women of the Bible and What He Wants to Do with You.* Nelson Books.

Richards, S. P., & Richards, L. (1999). *Every woman in the Bible.* T. Nelson.

Walton, A., & Walton, S. (2018). What Men Should Know About Women? In *The Window to Understanding and Building Healthy Relationships* (pp. 25-26).

Walton Publishing.

www.ingramcontent.com/pod-product-compliance
Lightning Source LLC
Chambersburg PA
CBHW061944220426
43662CB00012B/2017